POETR

COMMOTION

Couplets on Covid

from The Perky Poet

Nanda Marchant

COPYRIGHT

ISBN-13: 9798553825775

ISBN-10: 1477123456

Cover design by: Art Painter

Library of Congress Control Number: 2018675309

Printed in the United States of America

CONTENTS

DEDICATION

FOREWORD

FEBRUARY 1

MARCH 5

APRIL 11

MAY 25

JUNE 35

JULY 43

AUGUST 51

SEPTEMBER 57

OCTOBER 63

ACKNOWLEDGEMENTS 69

ABOUT THE AUTHOR 71

DEDICATION

To Tony, Hannah and Brenda, for encouraging my efforts and suffering my poetry recitals over the years as my alter egos: Pam Flayres and The Perky Poet

To Dickens (for some shameful plagiarism below)

And, of course to all the NHS staff and other hidden heroes who have gone above and beyond at this time:

It is a far, far better thing that you do now

Than you have ever done

It is a far, far bigger test of you

Than you have ever known

FOREWORD

Dear reader

Thank you for dipping your nose into this light-hearted look at 2020 through my eyes, AKA The Perky Poet. The pandemic has brought such heartache and loneliness to many that, rather than add to the misery, I wanted to try and lift the spirits and bring a little hope with my tongue-in-cheek perspective on events. From the madness of panic buying loo rolls, to the sadness of botched home-haircuts, I have tried to chronicle the mood and the mayhem month by month as events have unfolded.

At time of printing, a Covid-free future still looks a long way off. In the meantime I hope I can give you a smile and help you do what us Brits do best, ie: keep a sense of humour (albeit a rather dark and warped one at times!)

Nanda Marchant

November 2020

FEBRUARY

Early February

Worrying signs were there, but I think at this early point we were still all living in a dream world where we believed that what had been happening in China was still so very far away ... certainly distant from me in a sleepy little village in Leicestershire. Yet there was definitely a feeling of foreboding

Premonition

Interpret headlines best you can

Something strange afoot in Wuhan

Something wicked this way comes

To knobble me and all my chums

MARCH

Early March

It seems a lifetime ago when I started to seriously put pen to paper in the spring. I was obviously way over-optimistic with my presumption back then that it could be plain sailing by July, but I think few of us could imagine what was to come …

Fast forward to July

We are down at the pub in a wild celebration
Freedom at last after self-isolation
Enjoying a laugh with our dearest of friends
Time for cold lager* and summer weekends

[*A sensible move has been made by the owner
Who's taken off tap his usual Corona]
Though April and May were lonesome and bleak
We're now at a time when the bug's passed its peak

So tonight here we are, breathing sighs of relief
With a few tears of joy after moments of grief
For we've lost ones we loved, and some jobs are in tatters
But also we've learned what in life really matters:

We stopped being selfish and thought about others
Held tight** to our children, our parents and brothers
[**Metaphorically speaking – we did keep our distance
And kept washing hands, sanitised with persistence]

continued …

.../continued

We offered up loo roll that once we'd have stashed
Held onto our nerve when pension funds crashed
Helped little old ladies who needed some shopping
Even when illness showed no signs of stopping

As the virus took hold and quickened its pace
Those struck down stayed home eating pancakes and plaice
A strange combination, not eaten before
But 'twas all that our folks could slide under the door

We stifled the boredom with jigsaws and books
Stopped haircuts and waxing, gave up on our looks
For banned were the hairdresser, spa, gym and nails
So we slouched and got lazy, avoiding the scales

But tonight we don't care, and we've no need to hide
For we've learnt that what counts is not our outside
We may look like yetis, our pensions have dived
But break out the champers, at least we survived!

March 22nd

I found myself sorely missing my daughter at this time.

She was studying for her Masters as Covid hit, and stayed away for Mother's Day while we were isolating after my husband suspected he'd picked up the virus (and it turned out he had)

Mum's the word

A note to all on Mother's day

As your children stay away

The reason you may be apart

Is that you're deep inside their heart

This virus fills them with alarm

That precious mum may come to harm

So stay indoors, have virtual hugs

To try and minimise these bugs

Or if they visit, masked and gloved

Rest assured that you are loved xxx

Late March
One day it occurred to me how nature just seemed to carry on regardless of Corona, and maybe it was time to take more notice of it and count my blessings

Natural high

What does nature know of our plight?

The bees still buzz and the doves take flight

Daffodils grow and the clouds float by

The moon still rises in the sky

Crops push through and tilt in the breeze

Squirrels continue to peek from trees

Early blossoms share their scent

Sparrows chirp until they're spent

Though I may think my world has stopped

With all my privileges dropped

I'm starting to learn of life's true worth

And enjoy the beauty of mother earth

I see with fresh eyes this stunning place:

For free I can feel the sun on my face

Can listen to cows low in fields nearby

Take strength from the sight of a bright blue sky

Savour the smell of the rain and grass

And trust that this difficult time will pass

APRIL

Early April

As I started to go stir crazy, I came up with a few daft tips and home remedies to aid survival during lockdown

Life hacks

As all our supplies get increasingly low

Here's handy home tips to put <u>you</u> in the know

When shelves in your Asda are starting to lack

Do try improvising with one of my hacks:

I'm fresh out of loo roll, have used a dock leaf

It's ok I s'pose – rather rough underneath

My razor got blunt so sandpaper was used

It's left my poor legs feeling bloody and bruised

I've got low on dairy, am milking the cat

The scratches I've got show her views about that

I ran out of hand cream so tried mayonnaise

That tip worked a treat, mitts stayed silky for days

And hubby had hair straggling over his ears

But topiary worked, with the gardening shears

continued …

…/continued

Another thing missing because of this bug
Is a worldwide mass shortage of comforting hugs

But I've solved that one, I hope you'll think, on the whole
That we might somehow manage with gloves on a pole
It's not all depressing, some things don't run out:
Community spirit – there's plenty about

There's love, song and dancing, and dry British wit
Dark humour or daftness to make your sides split
There's plenty of tech to keep people in touch
And listening ears if you're needing a crutch

If your stash of good books is starting to dwindle
There's always the infinite joy of a Kindle
And if you've a bath, to put some fruit in
Happy days boys and girls, you can make your own gin

So take heart dear friends, we'll see this thing through
I've thought of some options, now over to you
If no inspiration, don't end up in tears
Just Google 'survival', 'Bear Grylls' or 'Ray Mears!'

I must have been feeling in a more sombre mood

when I wrote this one

Germ warfare

He coughs, and where the droplet lands

Is somewhere that you put your hands

You notice not, but touch your nose

And quietly inside it goes

Two days on, at shops you'll be

Wondering what to have for tea

So pick up things and put them back

Leaving germs on every pack

At the till you part with cash

Microbes transfer in a flash

And now in days the bug has spread

Long before you're ill in bed

So listen up, oh please don't roam

Heed advice and STAY AT HOME!

Early April

Remember clapping for NHS staff? We turned out every Thursday night and it was a rare moment when we got to wave to a neighbour, unless we happened to be putting the bins out at the same time. I wanted to remember other key workers too, so they get a mention here

Shout out to our heroes

A high five to our heroes, who'll help us see this through

They're more brave, in *my* view, than the likes of me and you

I'm talking of cashiers, sitting at the till

Helping with our shopping, as our germs we spill

There's all the docs and nurses, standing in harm's way

Giving every effort, for many hours a day

And I would like to thank you guys for emptying my bin

Keeping up with standards, while we are all locked in

There's MOT providers, keeping cars on roads

[Makes me feel inadequate, just writing little odes]

And what about the Hermes van, dropping off my packet

I take my hat off to you mate, I really couldn't hack it

Last night was for the NHS

We whooped, we cheered, we clapped

But here's a hug* for EVERYONE

Who's helping while we're trapped

(*virtual of course!)

Mid April

Most men have fairly short hair, so by mid to late April we were starting to see a few mullets and shaggy dogs, desperate for a trim. My husband was no exception, so I had a bash at it, with a rather blunt pair of kitchen scissors. He claims it wasn't too bad – I'm just thankful he couldn't see the back! I was inspired to try adding music to my poetry for once, so imagine this one sung to the tune of Scarborough Fayre

The haircut

I asked my man, should I cut your hair

Parsley sage rosemary and thyme

He cried no baby, please don't go there

It won't grow back, for qui-ite some time

I said a quick tidy is my only goal

Fear ye not, it will look sublime

I plan to use a nice pudding bowl

Furthermore, won't charge you a dime

The thought of this just sticks in my gullet

He repeated, numerous times

For I'll end up with an eighties mullet

And that would be a hideous crime

continued ...

…/continued

No just a snip around the ears

Trim on top, you'll lo-ook divine

And I can use the gardening shears

You'll be mown in next to no time

It didn't end well, harsh names I was called

Had to practice sev-eral times

He wouldn't sit still and now he is ba-ald

So please take heed from my little rhyme

And my thoughts turned to how I might manage with home salon treatments for myself too. Luckily, I have long hair in no specific style, so in truth, I managed to last out.

Drastic measures

My fringe was down to my armpits

My roots were silvery grey

When my daughter turned to me innocently

And said, with a smile, one day

'Mum – I've cut hair at uni

Us students have so little cash

Why don't you find me the scissors

Sit down and I'll give it a bash?'

With hairdressers closed in the crisis

I thought 'Well I've got little choice'

So I found myself saying 'go on then'

In a wary and trembling voice

'I might as well touch up your colour'

She added, producing a box

As I acquiesced, I then did my best

Not to fear for my poor little locks

continued …

It started out well with the hair dye
As she painted each strand, every follicle
My hair appeared fine, a deep shade of wine
But the bathroom looked quite diabolical
Her efforts at splashing on colour
Had sent streaks of red up the wall
Attempting to wipe, she'd left a great stripe
And I wasn't too happy at all

But what harm could she do with the trimming?
There was simply a fringe to get straight
Yet when I was cooked
I finally looked and realised I'd left it too late
In lining it up to my eyebrows
She'd left me no more than an inch
I'd hoped for a 'Sassoon' make-over
But ended up more like the Grinch

My warning to those feeling tempted:
If you don't want such stories to tell
Don't let the kids loose, to give you a spruce
You're better off 'au naturelle'!

Mid April

My husband was missing his 'no grey, no play' football cronies.
They hadn't had a game for weeks by this time

But they managed to come up with an alternative to keep
themselves entertained and slake that thirst for a pint and some
mindless blokey talk

The short walk home

'Right, I'm off to the Crown then'

Said hubby, all full of cheer

I know it's the second time this week

But I'm desperate for a beer

Peeved that he was leaving

But not one to cause a rift

I slapped on a smile and sweetly asked

If he'd be needing a lift

But he shrugged 'no' politely

And sauntered off with a swagger

He was only going to the study

So not far back to stagger

continued …

…/continued

Firing up the laptop
He relaxed in his cosy room
Clicked to join the virtual pub
And chat to his mates on Zoom

It's not too bad as a night out
You can chat, do a quiz, play bridge
OK, there's no pint from the landlord
But you only need pop to the fridge

Thus another good night of male bonding
Was had as they chatted and laughed
But he still missed the taste of cold lager
Poured fresh from a pump on dratt

He soon asked me 'Fancy a cellar?
I'll dig one for you as a gift'
The look on my face gave the answer
Now there WILL be a marital rift!

This is the kind of little ditty that pops into my head
when I can't sleep. I'm getting too old to remember anything
much longer than this without writing it down!

A short talk

Can we stop for a chatter?
What's wrong with a natter?
Well you may be spreading your germs
If you're six feet away
With a mask, well OK
I'm sorry, but those are my terms

It took me a while to get used to the mantra 'keys, phone, money, mask' when leaving the house, and even now, after all this time, do sometimes get caught out.

This thought crossed my brain one day as I put away a pair of skimpy undies ...

Oops!

Home made mask?

Need you ask?

Know it looks wrong

Cos it's a thong

Went out to roam

Left mask at home

Then got chastised

So improvised!

MAY

Early May

We were all starting to understand what amazing sacrifices some were making. My little odes seemed paltry compared to the heroics of many others, and inadequate to express the enormous gratitude I felt, Yet I hoped I was at least raising a smile or lifting the spirits, and writing helped keep me sane

Gratitude

These are the times when we have to stay safe

Even though we may argue and chafe

These are the days that we need to stay home

Despite our desire to travel and roam

These are the staff who have big risks to take

Keeping things running though their lives are at stake

These are the brave who are willing to dare

To look after old people and show that they care

These are the farmers, ensuring we're fed

Milking the cows while we're tucked up in bed

These are the firms we can view with affection

Who offer free content or means of connection

continued ...

…/continued

These are civil servants just doing their best

Their efforts continually put to the test

These are decisions unprecedented, tough

When whatever's decided will not be enough

These are machines that are making the masks

For nurses performing their life-saving tasks

These are the innovators breaking the rules

To bring us the vaccines, equipment and tools

These are the heroes who've lain down their lives

And now they are lost to their husbands, their wives

These are the angels to whom we're in debt

Whose sacrifices we must never forget

These are my words, and inadequate way

To give thanks for a debt I can never repay

I am luckily at the age where my daughter can quite happily look after herself, but at this point my heart went out to all those trying to juggle small children or cope with home-schooling during the education shut-down. I was especially thinking of single parents, as I was one for a long time and know I would have struggled to cope …

Single mum

She really needs three pairs of hands

As on the keyboard porridge lands.

She tells herself 'keep calm, come on, you've got this'

For wriggling, fractious on her lap

Sits her cheeky little chap,

Spilling breakfast all over her office

Did they take her for a fool

When they said 'Now please home school

Your toddler and your four year old, it's easy

Even though they're little yobs,

You can also do your job

From home' … No wonder she felt queasy

continued …

…/continued

She had no choice, as we can see,

But Jessica now needs a wee,

While Arthur's nappy whiffs and feels quite dirty

Yet does he care?

No he sits there

And jams his porridge right into her QWERTY

Her nerves are frayed, she battles on,

A work persona she must don

So clicks on 'Teams' and starts her morning meeting,

But Arthur's having none of it,

He's got more food, the little git

And flings a fistful at the screen in greeting

So when they said 'It can be done,

To work from home is so much fun'

They maybe didn't think of kids like Arthur,

Whose mum must juggle many plates,

She has no time for fancy dates

And wonders: 'Where the hell's his absent father?'

VE Day 8/5

It just came home to me on VE day how much we have to be thankful for, when comparing our circumstances to six years of war. I thought it would be nice to write a little ode to celebrate this special day

Then and now

At the end of the war, back in 45

The nation, relieved, thought 'Thank God we're alive'

After many lives dashed, and so much true sorrow

Young soldiers who'd lost their dreams of tomorrow.

Fighting in trenches in some awful place

Lucky to make it alive back to base

In such dark days, parents dreamed of times better,

But thousands received that condolence letter.

Yet many won medals and proved they were brave

In time, with their courage, our lives they would save.

Hidden heroes emerged: The Bletchley code breakers

Others kept us all fed, be it butchers or bakers.

continued …

…/continued

While housewives donned wellies and made a firm pledge
To do their bit too, and dig up our veg

After years of real hardship and fighting the hun
The moment at last when we did it, we won!

As news spread like wildfire they danced in the street,
And people were hugging whoever they'd meet

They drank and they cheered with exuberant passion,
The only big drawback – 'twas all still on ration.

So how did they feast, did they borrow and beg
For a bit of home brew or some cake with dried egg?

We're more blessed today for we've warm scones and beer,
Plus loo rolls and pasta to bring us some cheer.

So let's thank our luck, those guys had it so bleak –
They did six years of shutdown, we've just done six weeks!

Late May

As rules started to ease just the teensiest bit and we were allowed to go outside and meet someone at a distance in a park, it was wonderful to see my good friend Shaz. Pubs and shops were still closed, as were public toilets, plus we had picked a chilly day, so we were reduced to improvising (and crossing our legs!), but it was still a treat

Bus shelter brew

I thought: 'The world's gone helter-skelter

Stopping in an old bus shelter

For a safely distanced meeting

We couldn't hug, so waved in greeting

It smelt of wee, I didn't care

Because my lovely friend was there,

And we'd been waiting for the day

When seeing a pal is deemed ok

This spot would do, though dark and sleazy

It sheltered us, as it was breezy

What a treat to see a mate

I'd even dressed up for the date

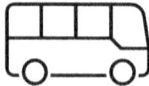

continued …

…/continued

Short sleeved dress, a touch of lippy
Regretted it, as then was nippy
So quickly broke out flask of tea
And balanced biccies on me knee

Glad the weather didn't scupper
Plans to meet and have a cuppa
And with pubs closed, this had to do
Couldn't stop long, there was no loo!

As venues go, it may sound bleak
Yet was my highlight of the week
Indeed the world is helter-skelter
But life's OK when we find shelter

JUNE

Early June

I'm sure what some people really started to miss quite quickly was physical contact with another human being

Old people and those living alone must have been climbing the walls from lack of contact and I was desperate to give my mum a hug for sure

Let's get physical

The big wide world needs a big wide hug

If only it weren't for the Covid bug

This thing has brought us to our knees

And we really need a heartfelt squeeze

A grandma's touch, or a hand to hold

But it passes on germs so we've been told

It makes me sad, unloved and glum

When I'm banned from a cutch with my lovely mum

I can't give a mate a friendly squidge

And I'm left feeling cold as my LG fridge

When I'm forced to connect in a 'virtual way'

So roll on the moment we can hug some day

Mid June

Though some local pubs offered take-away alternatives to the usual Friday night out, it just wasn't the same. We really started to miss sitting down at a nice pub or restaurant and enjoying a lovely meal. So this was a nostalgic wish for my favourite dish

Those were the days

Those were the days when we went to the pub
We just sat right down and relished our grub
We'd all pile in to a big bowl of dips
And a wandering hand might steal your chips
We loved the Friday night, after-work crowd
Where the bevvies were cold and the banter was loud
A queue at the loo, and a scrum at the bar
We were all packed in at The Crown or The Star
Oh halcyon days, where are you now?
For we can't go to The Lion, The Plough
All we can get is a sanitised box
With a take-away in, to avoid the pox
We're told: 'Thirty quid please including tax
But before you pay, here's our antibax'
So I long for the moment I'm back in the pub
I'm no big drinker but I love my grub
When it's served with finesse, appetizing and hot
Not tepid and sweaty in a plasticky pot
Oh bring me the lamb shanks, the jus-covered duck
Into sizzling fajitas I'll readily tuck
As for home cooking, I've now had my fill
And for crispy pork belly I'M READY TO KILL!

Mid June

I put my back out gardening, quite early in lockdown, and was struggling to get to the osteopath at first.

I hoped yoga might help, so looked up a variety of YouTube videos to help develop some sort of technique. I won't even mention how the Bhangra went!

Lockdown yoga

I started YouTube yoga

To limber up my joints

'But was it such a good idea?'

I've thought at certain points

I'm hopeless at the Down Dog

My hamstrings poor at stretching

With bottom pointed in the air

I never look that fetching

I tried to do a head stand

But that I failed to knobble

My legs were flailing uncontrolled

My fat began to wobble

continued …

.../continued

I had a go at Warrior
My stance would make you cringe
Especially when I lunged too hard
And felt my pelvis twinge

But some steps could be simpler
Which I'll consider maybe
I mean, what's not to like
In a move called Happy Baby?

And Corpse pose – that I've mastered
I just lie on my back
Start dribbling, then drop off to sleep
So think I've got the knack

Yet maybe yoga's not for me
Because: Oh bloomin 'eck
I've now been stuck for hours
With my foot behind my neck!

Having had Covid, my husband joined the plasma trial, as plasma was thought to help patients convalescing.

I'd like to have dedicated this little ode to him, but it was hard to rhyme with Tony!

Lockdown Limerick 1

There once lived a brave girl called Shona

Who caught a bad dose of Corona

Though she was quite sick

She bounced back real quick

Then thrived as a top plasma donor

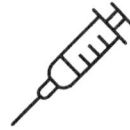

JULY

Early July

Throughout lockdown I've been conscious that people have had very different views on Covid, with some petrified and others much more gung-ho or philosophical about the risks. I'd say I'm somewhere in the middle, not an extreme anti-baxer nor one to flout the basic rules, and my husband has a similar attitude.

But I know for some families, opposing attitudes have caused heated arguments. This prompted me to put pen to paper, with a few names changed to protect the innocent!

Role reversal

Now here's the latest issue
That I feel compelled to mention
Different household attitudes to Covid
Causing tension
A husband's agoraphobic
And a'fearing for his life
But the kids are acting wayward
And he can't hold back his wife
Although he's barred the doorway
A he's the one who's stronger
It's led to a big showdown
As her locks get ever longer
The hairdressers are beckoning
She wants to take the risk
Leading to a tussle
Where the bloke nears slips a disc

.../continued

And then there's aged Elsie
Whose grandkids fuss and fiddle
So she declines to let them know
That she sneaked out to Lidl
She feels that she is sensible
And needs to have her way
It's sending her doolally
Stuck at home alone all day

It's not just other households
Who suffer such a plight
My eldest son drives me insane
Bleaching all in sight
I mention meeting with a friend
He really huffs at that
And on returning home
I'm firmly grilled on where I sat
'Were the windows open?
Did your fingers touch a cup?'
'Did you take the antibax?
You're sure you were masked up?'
I thought it was the younger kids
Who didn't give a damn
I didn't think that he would be
The member of the fam
To lecture me on every rule
And make me feel so hounded
PS: I'm writing in my room
Because I've now been grounded!

Mid July

At the start of lockdown I volunteered to do the shopping for a lovely local couple who were shielding. They were in their 70s and had met again a few years ago after being sweethearts when they were young

Hoping to tie the knot in the spring, their plans were scuppered when Covid hit. As rules relaxed, they managed a small wedding

He's a bit old to be carrying her over the threshold without doing his back in, and she wouldn't get away with a white dress, but they had a lovely romantic day. I was so pleased for them and wanted to write them a poem

Love in Lutterworth

This tale is of Maggie, a fair maid from Lutters

Cursed by Corona, her wedding in tatters

Her beau, after years, had asked for her hand

Then lockdown came in and nuptials were banned

Yes Alan, a twitcher, had wooed his love-bird

But a formal 'I do' just couldn't be heard

He'd plucked up the courage and got on one knee

But months stuck indoors meant it wasn't to be

continued …

…/continued

Now at last lovely Maggie can stand by his side

As the golf club plays host to a radiant bride

A few small adjustments they needed to ask

Saying 'please keep your distance and do bring a mask'

This didn't phase Mags for she answered to that:

'I've found one with sparkles that matches me hat

We can do without music, the pomp, and the doves

As long as we don't need to wear rubber gloves

The rest I can stand, but that rule was a shock

I just can't comply as they won't match me frock!'

The venue caved in and the bride had her way

So our story ends well, 'twas a fabulous day

The weather held good, they remembered the rings

Friends came and gifted them all sorts of things

Vows were exchanged, and cake eaten after

They lived long and happy, with life full of laughter

Love Nanda x

We are in the enviable position of enjoying lots of holidays, so feel extremely blessed. Nonetheless it was frustrating to have our plans cancelled, especially my husband's surprise 60th. So when we finally managed a little trip to the Czech Republic, we really appreciated our moment of freedom

Thwarted plans

This year we'd planned to slow it down
And take exciting trips
But after things shut down in March
We thought we'd had our chips
Our booking made for Serbia
A 60th surprise
Became the first one cancelled
Plans dissolved before our eyes

'Twas back on the agenda
When there came a little flurry
Of countries with a 'corridor'
We rebooked in a hurry
With Belgrade looking promising
But then the FCO
Decided that, with riots there
We could no longer go

'We're still the lucky ones' we felt
We've also got a ticket
For Italy, September which
We thought a safer wicket

continued …

.../continued

So something to look forward to
But then to our disgust
We learnt that our provider sadly
Went and bit the dust

It felt like we were fated
But we chose, with trepidation
To not throw in the towel
Or opt for a staycation
Instead we searched to find a place
Where Covid still was low
So plumped for lovely Czechia
And little-trod Brno

We followed all the guidance
Washing hands, masks on the plane
And what a lovely trip it was
I now feel far more sane
I know some think it's risky
And the fallout could be chronic
But leaving these four walls for once
Was truly such a tonic

The beer was great, the weather warm
The castles quite enchanted
Plus lesson learnt, to never take
My freedom so for granted!

AUGUST

August
By this time I hadn't earned a penny for six months.
I started wondering wistfully if there was another way …

A change of career?
'What can I do with work dead for now?'
Is the regular thought that furrows my brow
Since Corona came the phone's gone quiet
I've slowed right down and failed to diet
Felt quite listless (though done every chore)
And reached a point where my mind needs more
I've brainstormed ideas for a fun new role
Though I'm far too old to gyrate that pole
The weight's crept on – my resolve is shoddy
So I'd make precious little from selling my body
I can't trade art that's quirky or quaint
As I'm not artistic, don't scribble or paint
And I'm no inventor of miracle drugs
Won't make a bomb curing Covid or bugs
Not sporty enough for a personal trainer
But, wait! I've got it, it's quite a no-brainer
After years of hard work, why _should_ I aspire
To decades more slog when I could retire?
I can simply write ditties, for a bit of commission
Or do the occasional stage rendition
And while I suspect the pay would be crappy
Penning birthday card verses may make me happy
So I'll send hubby out to earn that crust
While for me, boys and girls, it's Clintons or bust!

This short ditty was inspired by the sudden surge in city-dwellers deciding to move out to the countryside, where Corona rates tend to be lower

Lockdown Limerick 2

I knew of a country farm owner

Kept himself to himself, a real loner

But he swiftly had 'mates'

From the town at his gates

As they knew they'd be safe there from 'Rona

The government do love a good campaign slogan and this was a catchy one. I know added rules became a bit of a muddle by this time, but some people couldn't even seem to follow the basics

Hands … Face … Space cadets?

Yeah I'm a minor rebel
I like to break a rule
It started in my childhood
At a straight-laced grammar school
I may not wait for the little green man
Prefer to jay walk if I can
Another of my mild offences
Once stuck champers on expenses
Yeah I'm a minor rebel and I like to think I'm cool

Yeah I'm a minor rebel
But some diktats I follow
They're easy rules to flout
Yet the victory would be hollow
A favourite one across these lands
Is you must often wash your hands
Another, not too much to ask
Is, shopping, you should wear a mask
Upon yer face, not under-chin
(As useless there as in the bin)

continued …

.../continued

Yeah I'm a minor rebel

But these rules ain't hard to swallow

There are other minor rebels, but some of tiny brain

No matter how you spell it out and ask them to refrain:

Keep your distance, save a life

Don't cause a spike and risk your wife

Scrub those hands and don those masks

But some won't do these simple tasks

They may be minor rebels but I wish they'd think again!

SEPTEMBER

Late September

I couldn't believe the headlines when Covid cases started rising rapidly and the supermarket shelves were suddenly emptied of toilet rolls again.

You can rest assured Aldi will have something useful in its middle aisles come rain or shine though

Supermarket Sweep – 28/9

So would they panic buy again?
'Twas not a case of if, but when
It started early yesterday
When toilet roll just rolled away

Then tinned tomatoes all ran low
I drew a blank in TESCO so
I turned to WAITROSE in a huff
But they were low on other stuff

For tins and bread I didn't look far
But they were out of best foie gras
And women fought like seasoned mobsters
Over two remaining lobsters

They'd put a limit on quails' eggs
Leaving me with just the dregs
ALDI was a different story
Got some goodies, felt the glory

continued ...

.../continued

But there I saw a pair of fools
Stocking up on paddling pools
While there's no issue finding crumpets
The store has put a cap on trumpets

You're OK when buying rice
But welding kits sell in a trice
So pop in quick for your 'best buys'
Things disappear before your eyes

For me, I feel: 'Let's stop this madness
Panic buying leads to sadness
I'll just think: 'Who gives a damn?
There's always that old tin of Spam
I can soon blow off the dust
And face Fray Bentos if I must!

Early September

Around this time a story hit the press about some Covidiot who managed to get around the rules on his flight home, by eating throughout the entire journey – nobody thought you were clever mate :(

Lockdown limerick 3

Last week saw a fool on a plane

Who thought wearing masks was a pain

The whole way he ate Pringles

So, maskless, could mingle

Hope you're banned in revenge, you pea brain!

And here I was just thinking about how little I get out these days …

Lockdown limerick 4

Since the start of this blasted Corona

I've become a regular loner

Rarely getting about

My last grand day out

Was my slot as a local blood donor!

An article in the Times made me think about the demise of high fashion at the moment – with a lot of people content to work in their joggy-bottoms or not bother with make-up. That's certainly true for me, though I haven't let standards slip as badly as I allude to here!

Sartorial Slouch

'Has Covid killed sexy?' a newspaper asks
Now that our beauty is covered in masks
I tend to agree, as it's something I've felt
When stuck behind fabric, my make-up a-melt
Foundation rubs off, gets clingy and drippy
Plus what is the point of that bright glossy lippy?

'Go for sexy attire' – An alternate suggestion
But one that seems pointless and out of the question
You can't rock an entrance in heels, through a room
When most of your meetings are held over Zoom
And nor can you cheekily flash a bare calf
When all that's on camera's your face and top half

Instead I've gone comfy and thrown out my Spanx
They conspire to constrict all my wobbles - no thanks
I've fully embraced a life lived in joggers
And turned all 'authentic' like some lifestyle vloggers
Hope others embrace the TRUE ME underneath
And hey, I'm so chilled I've stopped brushin' me teeth!

OCTOBER

Early October

I can't believe how many new words and expressions related to Covid have come into our vocabulary this year, many of them featuring on front page news

It's been tricky, but I've managed to turn a full alphabet of words and headlines into an ode, though a fair amount had to end up on the cutting room floor, as I couldn't cram it all in – it also made for a bit of dodgy rhyming and scanning I'm afraid!

A-Z of Covid

Antibodies keep the virus out

Barnard Castle's a good day out

Bleach is best says orange Trump

Bojo's dad has been a chump

Clapping … **C**hina … **C**onvalesce

Death rate up – oh what a mess

Epidemic or pandemic? **E**ither way you lose

Furlough, **F**ever, **F**ace masks help, though Donald says

Fake news'

Granny's gorn … **G**loves must be worn …

Gove fails at party unity

Hygiene's key … **H**azmat shortage …

Here comes **H**erd Immunity

Jigsaws sell out … **J**obs are lost …

Joe Wicks plays his part

continued …

…/continued

Killer virus getting worse so

Keep 2M apart

Long Covid … Loss of smell … panic buying Loo rolls

Mental health is suffering … Marcus sets new meal goals

Nurses getting burnout … protect the NHS

Online meetings pave the way to sloppy state of dress

Plasma trials … PPE … Persistent cough's a worry

Quarantine. Don't stand in

Queues – book online slots, but hurry!

Remdesivir's the answer, or is it? … Rule of six

Stay at home … Self-isolate plus Shielding's in the mix

Support bubbles keep people sane … but

Swabs we sometimes lack

Statistics Show a Spike in deaths but good news …

Strictly's back

Track & Trace means Trillions spent … Tier 1, Tier 2, Tier 3

Unemployment on the rise, Unhappiness we'll see

Vaccines coming soon they say … Viral load's what counts

Wuhan's Where it all began, with bats by all accounts

Xtra funding needed … can X-Factor return?

Yoga's one of many skills that we can all home learn

Zoom's become the way to meet

Their shares just keep ascending

Phew, at last that's over, it was almost never-ending!

I'd like to finish on a note of hope. I was thinking ahead to Christmas and imagining it might be a bit of a damp squib this year.

But I couldn't finish on a downer, so here is my wish for you all. Stay safe!

Covid Chrimbo

Late October

I wonder what Christmas will bring us this year

That usual time for tinsel and cheer

When friends may turn up, smiley faced at our doors

With gifts and mince pies held aloft in their paws

Our homes look inviting, the tree is bedecked

And rellies stuff faces or drink til they're wrecked

There's turkey to carve and crackers to pull

Plus letters to Santa and stockings crammed full

The kids get spoiled rotten and diets are blown

As we overindulge on a huge Toblerone

continued ...

.../continued

Christmas day afternoon

The big day was dismal I've got to confess
The black cloud of Covid created some stress
Being socially-distanced left me feeling glum
No family crowd, just hubby and mum
Great boxes of crackers were left on the shelves
The 'rule of six' meaning we didn't need twelves
Our fat golden turkey? Afraid no such luck
We sat there forlorn with the scrawniest duck
No visit from Santa, no reindeer for me
As our little village was deemed a 'Tier 3'

Christmas day evening

We waved bye to mother, deflated, subdued
Having drunk little wine and just picked at our food
Imagine our shock when she came back a-knocking
To say: 'I've forgotten to give you your stocking
It was popped in the car, days ago, sanitized
So it's now quarantined – only just realised'
'I'm too old for stockings' I wanted to say
'And how could you truly lift spirits today?'
But my fears were all groundless, how wrong I had been
Cos I undid the wrapper and got the vaccine!

ACKNOWLEDGEMENTS

I am so thankful to have had the opportunity to 'pedal my wares' over the years to long-suffering friends, family and work colleagues who will listen and politely laugh in all the right places when I decide to get lyrical and test out my work on them.

Particular thanks should go to those kind listeners, and also those who have entrusted into my hands the task of creating something unique for their birthday or wedding celebration, be it a rap, a song, an ode, or even the occasional funeral reading. I hope I didn't let them down.

I should also make mention of Crick Drama Group and the West Haddon Players, both of whom have indulged me over the years when I've written sketches and ditties to perform on stage, muscling in on their variety shows to insist I got a slot.

The national press should get a mention as one of the dailies printed two of my poems, giving me a much-needed confidence boost. They shall remain nameless, as while I'm so grateful, in truth I'd have preferred the Times, who unfortunately turned their noses up!

And finally, I need to repeat my gratitude to my husband Tony who pushed me to 'stop thinking small' and to just get on and publish this thing. Thanks for your unwavering fandom. You are my loved and unsung hero.

ABOUT THE AUTHOR

Nanda has always loved anything to do with the written and spoken word. As a language graduate who went on to live abroad for some years, she delights in not only wrapping her tongue around the English language, but also French and to a lesser degree Spanish, plus some rather ropey Italian and Dutch.

By day, Nanda works for herself as a market research consultant, interviewing all sorts of interesting types. She then has to make sense of what they say, writing reports and presenting the findings, all of which play to her love of meeting new people, writing a good story and performing to a crowd.

By evening, she might be learning lines for a play on the local stage (increasingly hard as she gets older) or writing a sketch or poem to perform.

By night, she could well be tossing and turning, unable to sleep until she has a ditty down on paper that has been rotating round her head.

By marriage, she has a husband and grown up daughter

And by the end, she will still likely have a pen, mobile, or laptop by her side, ready to jot down her latest rhyme!

www.nandamarchant.com

Printed in Great Britain
by Amazon